Aunt Phil's Trunk

Teacher Guide

for

The Spell of the Yukon and Other Verses

Poetry by
ROBERT SERVICE

Curriculum by
LAUREL DOWNING BILL

Teacher Guide

for

The Spell of the Yukon And Other Verses

Poetry By
Robert Service

Curriculum By
Laurel Downing Bill

Special thanks to Nicole Cruz for her assitance in makng this teacher guide and its accompanying student workbook for *The Spell of the Yukon and Other Verses*

COPYRIGHT 2017
Reprinted 2023

Aunt Phil's Trunk LLC
Anchorage, Alaska
www.AuntPhilsTrunk.com

ISBN: 978-1-940479-20-0

Instructions for using Aunt Phil's Trunk Proudly Presents *The Spell of the Yukon And Other Verses* Curriculum

This curriculum is designed to be used as part of a ninth- or tenth-grade Language Arts curriculum. In each lesson, students will learn new vocabulary words, answer discussion questions and consider how concepts such as rhyme scheme, theme, tone and imagery are used in each poem. At the conclusion of every lesson, students will complete an enrichment activity to encourage deeper interaction with the poem, as well as practice writing their own poetry.

After reading and analyzing more than 30 of Robert Service's famous poems, students will read two chapters about his life and complete a final lesson analyzing how his life events impacted his poetry.

I hope that you and your students enjoy this journey into the life and poetry of Robert Service.

GRADING: Grading instructions and Rubric grids for each lesson begins on page 121.

NOTE:

Teachers/parents – Please note that some of Robert Service's poems are about the shady side of life during the Klondike Gold Rush.

TABLE OF CONTENTS

TABLE OF CONTENTS (Con't.)

Robert Service Cabin, Dawson

Courtesy Alaska State Library

THE SPELL OF THE YUKON

LESSON 1: THE LAND GOD FORGOT

VOCABULARY

Look for these words in your reading:

Desolate – abandoned
Gaunt – grim or forbidding
Insensate – lacking humane feelings
Abysmal – extremely bad

READING

Read: To C.M., the Introduction and "The Land God Forgot" (Pages 3-10)

DISCUSSION QUESTIONS

1) Who was C.M.? Why did Robert Service dedicate the *Spell of the Yukon and Other Verses* to her?
According to biographer Enid Mallory, C.M. stands for Constance MacLean of Vancouver, British Columbia. In his book, titled Under the Spell of the Yukon, Mallory said the 28-year-old Service had become infatuated with the young lady when they met in Duncan, B.C., in 1902. (Page 3)

2) Did Robert Service ever return to the Yukon cabin that he wrote about in "Good-bye Little Cabin" after he wrote the poem in 1912? What happened to that cabin?
Robert Service never returned to that cabin after he left the Yukon. The cabin has been turned into a place for visitors to learn more about Robert Service. (Page 4)

3) In your own words, describe the land that Robert Service wrote about in "The Land God Forgot."
Answers will vary. The land is barren, quiet, scary, cursed and lonely.

4) Have you ever been to a place that resembles the land in "The Land God Forgot"? If so, explain why the poem reminds you of that place. *(Answers will vary)*

FAVORITE QUOTE

What is your favorite line from "The Land God Forgot." Why? *(Answers will vary)*

ENRICHMENT ACTIVITY

Using some of the words that you used to describe the land in Discussion Question 3, write your own poem describing a place that you have been or an imaginary setting.

THE SPELL OF THE YUKON

LESSON 2: THE SPELL OF THE YUKON

VOCABULARY
Look for these words in your reading:

Shun – to avoid purposely
Caribou – a large animal of the deer family
Bludgeons – beats, thrashes
Luring – to tempt or attract

READING
Read: "The Spell of the Yukon" (Pages 11-13)

DISCUSSION QUESTION

1) What appears to draw the narrator to the Yukon at the beginning of the poem?
Gold first drew the narrator to the Yukon. (Page 11)

2) What draws the narrator to the Yukon at the end of the poem?
The beauty and peace of the Yukon became the draw by the end of the poem. (Page 13)

3) Does the narrator love everything about the Yukon? Explain your answer.
No. He says you hate it at first and calls it hell. The winters are hard and scary. He's tried to leave it behind, but he keeps getting pulled back. (Pages 11-13)

4) Does the narrator live in the Yukon? How can you tell?
No, the narrator does not live in the Yukon. He talks about going back there several times in the poem. (Page 13)

5) If you had to describe the moral or lesson of "The Spell of the Yukon," what would it be?
Answers will vary. One example may be that there are more important things in life than gold.

FAVORITE QUOTE

What is your favorite line from "The Spell of the Yukon"? Why? *(Answers will vary)*

ENRICHMENT ACTIVITY

Robert Service used an alternate rhyme scheme in "The Spell of the Yukon" making it very easy to read. We also call this the ABAB pattern because the last word in each line of the stanza rhymes with the last word in the alternating line. For example:

There's gold, and it's haunting and haunting; (A)
It's luring me on as of old; (B)
Yet it isn't the gold that I'm wanting (A)
So much as just finding the gold. (B)

Write your own poem using an alternate rhyme scheme.

THE SPELL OF THE YUKON

LESSON 3: THE HEART OF THE SOURDOUGH

VOCABULARY

Look for these words in your reading:

Sourdough – Alaskan term for a person who has spent at least one winter north of the Arctic Circle

Tundra – a treeless plain especially of arctic regions having a permanently frozen layer below the surface

Defy – openly resist or refuse to obey

Flouted – ignore in a disrespectful way

READING

Read: "The Heart of the Sourdough" (Pages 14-15)

DISCUSSION QUESTION

1) According to the narrator, what is important to the heart of a sourdough?
Answers will vary. The heart of a sourdough longs for adventure and conflict. It wants a life that is uncomplicated, but hard. It is drawn to the Northland and everything about it.

2) What battle does the narrator describe in the poem? Who will win the fight?
He describes a fight between himself and the Wild. The Wild will eventually win. (Page 15)

3) What do you think the narrator meant by the line below?
"I long for a whiff of bacon and beans, a snug shakedown in the snow; a trail to break, and a life at stake, and another bout with the foe."
Answers will vary. The narrator longs for the life of adventure that he finds in the North. He has grown tired and bored of the easy life that he has found elsewhere. (Page 15)

4) Does "The Heart of the Sourdough" remind you of another poem or story? If so, which one? *(Answers will vary)*

FAVORITE LINE

What is your favorite line from "The Heart of the Sourdough"? Why?
(Answers will vary)

ENRICHMENT ACTIVITY

How would you describe your heart? What people, places and things are most important to you? Make a list of 5-10 things. Write a poem using your list.

THE SPELL OF THE YUKON

LESSON 4: THE THREE VOICES

VOCABULARY

Look for these words in your reading:

Aloft – at a great height
Anthem – a song or hymn of praise or gladness
Sally – an excursion
Unfurled – to unfold

READING

Read: "The Three Voices" (Page 16)

DISCUSSION QUESTION

1) Who do the three voices belong to?
The three voices belong to the waves, wind and stars. (Page 16)

2) What do the three voices tell the narrator?
The waves tell stories of the open ocean, populous cities and men who have sought after gold. The wind teaches a lesson of staying free from the love of gold and to love nature. The stars sing a song of the glory of God, man and a wondrous plan. (Page 16)

3) What does the narrator long for?
"I long for the peace of the pine-gloom, when the scroll of the Lord is unfurled, and the wind and the wave are silent, and world is singing to world." (Page 16)

4) Can you relate to the narrator's experience on the beach? If so, how?
(Answers will vary)

FAVORITE LINE

What is your favorite line from "The Three Voices"? Why?
(Answers will vary)

ENRICHMENT ACTIVITY

Robert Service often spent time walking outdoors with pen and paper to write about whatever he saw and experienced. Spend some time outdoors writing down what you see, smell, hear, touch, etc. Write a poem that shares this experience.

THE SPELL OF THE YUKON

LESSON 6: THE PARSON'S SON

VOCABULARY

Look for these words in your reading:

Toiled – long strenuous fatiguing effort
Squandered – spent extravagantly or foolishly
Malamute – a sled dog of northern North America
Fiendish – extremely cruel or wicked

READING

Read: "The Parson's Son" (Pages 22-25)

DISCUSSION QUESTION

1) How would you describe the Parson's son? What did he look like?
"...been snow-blind twice; look where my foot's half gone; and that gruesome scar on my left cheek, where the frost-fiend bit to the bone." (Page 22)

2) How many years did he spend in the Yukon? Why did he go there?
He spent twenty years in the Yukon mining for gold. (Pages 22 and 24)

3) What happened to the Parson's son?
He died in his bunk alone and hunger-maddened malamutes tore him flesh from bone. (Page 25)

4) At the end of the poem we learn that the Parson's son died alone on his bunk. Judging from his song, do you think that he had a happy life in the Yukon? Why or why not?
(Answers will vary)

FAVORITE LINE

What is your favorite line from "The Parson's Son"? Why?
(*Answers will vary)*

ENRICHMENT ACTIVITY

Imagine that you are an old man or woman at the end of your life. Write a song that summarizes your life. Where did you go? What did you spend your life doing? Who was important to you?

THE SPELL OF THE YUKON

LESSON 7: THE CALL OF THE WILD

VOCABULARY

Look for these words in your reading:

Grandeur – awe-inspiring magnificence
Desolation – lifeless land
Hearken – listen; attend to
Veneer – a superficial or deceptively attractive appearance, display or effect

READING

Read: "The Call of the Wild" (Pages 26-28)

DISCUSSION QUESTIONS

1) What is the theme (central idea) of "The Call of the Wild"?
"The Call of the Wild" describes the powerful pull that the Northland has on those that continue to return despite the fact that it is a dangerous, lonely and desolate place.

2) What are five words you would use to describe a person that hears the call of the wild?
Answers will vary. Some examples include: adventurous, nature loving, curious, spontaneous, wild, carefree, bold, strong and daring.

3) What are some differences that you noticed in the style of this poem compared to the other Robert Service poems that you have studied so far?
He uses a series of questions to describe the characteristics of the wild and those that are called to it.

4) What feelings and emotions did this poem elicit in you? Go back and reread the poem. Can you pinpoint specific elements, words, or lines that caused these emotions?
Answers will vary.

FAVORITE LINE

What is your favorite line from "The Call of the Wild"? Why?
(*Answers will vary)*

ENRICHMENT ACTIVITY

Questions can be used as a literary device to create dramatic effect, persuade the audience or cause the reader to ponder an important theme. Write your own question poem that imitates the style of "The Call of the Wild."

THE SPELL OF THE YUKON

LESSON 8: THE LONE TRAIL

VOCABULARY

Look for these words in your reading:

Fain – in a willing manner
Drouth – long period of dry weather
Anguish – extreme pain or distress of the body or mind
Mirage – an optical illusion caused by atmospheric conditions, especially the appearance of a sheet of water in a desert or on a hot road caused by the refraction of light from the sky by heated air

READING

Read: "The Lone Trail" (Pages 29-30)

DISCUSSION QUESTIONS

1) Why do you think Robert Service titled this poem, "The Lone Trail"? Support your answer with a line from the poem.
Answers will vary. One example: The Lone Trail describes a path that is not traveled by many because it is risky, dangerous and different from the way that the rest of the world lives. "And somehow you're sick of the highway, with its noise and its easy needs, and you seek the risk of the by-way, and you reck not where it leads."

2) According to the narrator, why would some choose the lone trail over the other trails?
The lone trail is one of adventure that lures one away from the safe, boring life.

3) Other than the words lone and trail, what word do you notice is used many times in this poem? Why do you think Robert Service used that word so often in the poem?
Service begins many lines with the word and. Explanations will vary, and they will learn more about this technique in the enrichment activity.

4) Reread "The Lone Trail." How can you relate it to your own life?
Answers will vary.

FAVORITE LINE

What is your favorite line from "The Lone Trail"? Why?
(*Answers will vary)*

ENRICHMENT ACTIVITY

Anaphora refers to a literary technique where successive lines begin with the same word or phrase. Poets have used this technique for centuries to create rhythm and intensify emotion. Anaphora has been used in a lot of religious writing, including biblical psalms, and in romantic writing, such as works by William Shakespeare. Find at least three poems that use anaphora and write the titles below.

1) ____
2) ____
3) ____

Compose a poem using anaphora.

THE SPELL OF THE YUKON

LESSON 9: THE PINES

VOCABULARY

Look for these words in your reading:

Niggard – stingy or ungenerous
Gelid – extremely cold
Aeons – a very long period of time
Legion – large military force

READING

Read: "The Pines" (Pages 31-32)

DISCUSSION QUESTIONS

1) A stanza is a group of lines within a poem that are typically set apart by a blank line. Reread the first stanza of the poem. How does it set the mood for the rest of the poem?
The first stanza of the poem creates a dark and gloomy mood. (Page 31)

2) What literary technique do you recognize in the third stanza of "The Pines"?
Anaphora. (Page 31)

3) What are five words that can be used to describe this poem? Some examples are: dark, gloomy or woods.
Answers will vary.

4) Judging by the first nine poems that we've studied, what topics and themes did Robert Service often write about?
Robert Service often wrote about nature, the Northland, the wild and the desire for adventure.

FAVORITE LINE

What is your favorite line from "The Pines"? Why?
Answers will vary.

ENRICHMENT ACTIVITY

Write a poem consisting of at least four stanzas that contain the words you chose in Discussion Question 3.

Spell of the Yukon Vocabulary

Crossword Puzzle I

Read the Across and Down clues and fill in the blank boxes that match the number on the clues

ACROSS

1 A song or hymn of praise or gladness
4 A very long period of time
6 Lacking physical, mental or moral vigor
8 Spent extravagantly or foolishly
11 In a willing manner
12 A sled dog of northern North America
13 Abandoned
14 Large military force
15 Lacking humane feelings
17 Long period of dry weather
21 A large animal of the deer family
23 Beats, thrashes
24 Listen; attend to
26 Awe-inspiring magnificence
27 Grim or forbidding
30 Firmness of mind or spirit
31 A superficial or deceptively attractive appearance, display or effect
32 Ignore in a disrespectful way
33 Openly resist or refuse to obey
34 To avoid purposely

DOWN

2 A treeless plain especially of arctic regions having permanently frozen layer below the surface
3 Long strenuous fatiguing effort
5 To unfold
7 Lifeless land
8 Alaskan term for a person who has spent at least one winter north of the Arctic Circle
9 Extremely cruel or wicked
10 An excursion
12 Of many and various kinds
16 Stingy or ungenerous
18 An optical illusion caused by atmospheric conditions, especially the appearance of a sheet of water in a desert or on a hot road caused by the refraction of light from the sky by heated air
19 Extremely bad
20 Strength of spirit
22 Extreme pain or distress of the body or mind
25 To tempt or attract
28 At a great height
29 Extremely cold

Spell of the Yukon Vocabulary

Crossword Puzzle I Key

Read the Across and Down clues and fill in the blank boxes that match the number on the clues

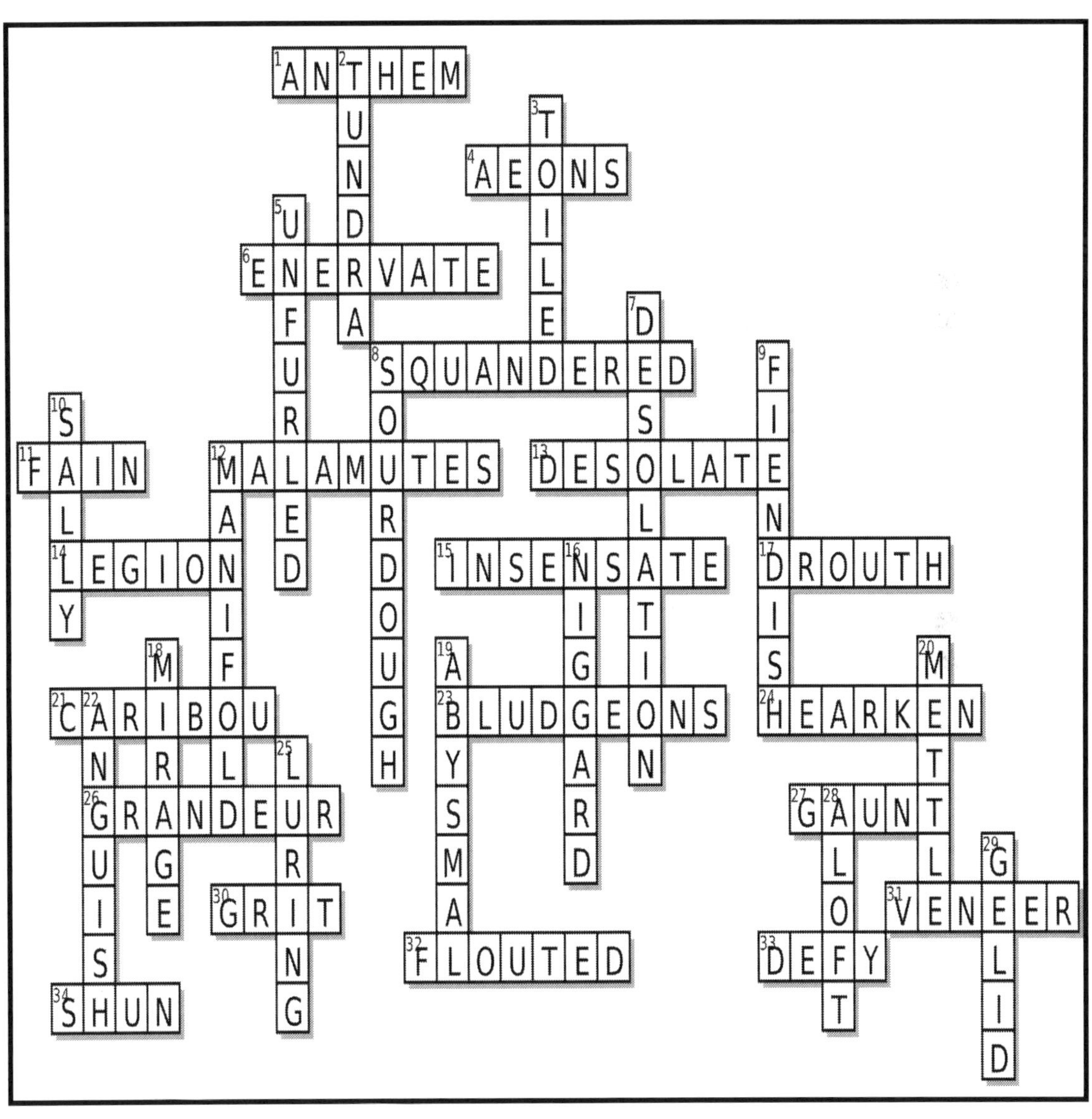

THE SPELL OF THE YUKON

LESSON 10: THE LURE OF LITTLE VOICES

VOCABULARY

Look for these words in your reading:

Stark – desolate
Sentinel – a guard whose job is to stand and keep watch
Mandate – an authoritative command
Comrade – close friend or associate

READING

Read: "The Lure of Little Voices" (Pages 33-34)

DISCUSSION QUESTIONS

1) Who is the audience of this poem? How do you know?
The audience is a woman who is very important to the speaker, most likely his wife. He refers to her as honey several times and says that the voices are telling him to leave her.

2) What are the little voices telling the speaker?
The little voices are telling the speaker to come to return to the wild.

3) Has the speaker been to the place that the little voices are calling him to? Explain your answer.
Yes. We know that he has been to the place that the voices are calling him because he says, "He was ours before you got him, and we want him once again." (Page 33)

4) In poetry, we can often read between the lines to make logical assumptions about what the poet is trying to get across to the reader. This is called an inference. Reread the poem and see what inference you can make.
Answers will vary.

FAVORITE LINE

What is your favorite line from "The Lure of Little Voices"? Why?
Answers will vary.

ENRICHMENT ACTIVITY

Write a poem in response to "The Lure of Little Voices" from the point of view of either:

1) The person that the speaker is speaking to in the poem.
2) The speaker. Respond to the little voices that are luring him to the wild.

THE SPELL OF THE YUKON

LESSON 11: THE SONG OF THE WAGE-SLAVE

VOCABULARY

Look for these words in your reading:

Shirk – to avoid something one ought to do
Repentant – state of repentance (feeling sorry for one's sins)
Wrought – work
Blaspheme – speak irreverently about God or sacred things

READING

Read: "The Song of the Wage-Slave" (Pages 35-37)

DISCUSSION QUESTIONS

1) Briefly summarize "The Song of the Wage-Slave"?
Answers will vary. The speaker is pleading his case with God. He has worked hard his whole life for God and wants to be judged by his hard work and not his sins.

2) Who is the wage-slave? Who is the Big Boss?
The wage-slave is the speaker who has worked hard his whole life for God. The Big Boss is God.

3) What does the wage-slave want?
All he wants is to rest from his work.

4) Can you relate to this poem in any way? Explain why or why not.
Answers will vary.

FAVORITE LINE

What is your favorite line from "The Song of a Wage-Slave"? Why?
(*Answers will vary)*

ENRICHMENT ACTIVITY

There are many things that we should look at when analyzing poetry. Three questions we should always ask are:

1) What is the poet saying?
2) What inferences can I make? (Read between the lines.)
3) How can I relate to this poem?

Choose a poem written by someone other than Robert Service, and then write your answers to the three questions above.

THE SPELL OF THE YUKON

LESSON 12: GRIN

VOCABULARY

Look for these words in your reading:

Clout – influence
Cultivate – try to acquire or develop (a quality, sentiment or skill)
Rebuff – to refuse or check sharply
Cuff – to strike with an open hand

READING

Read: "Grin" (Pages 38-39)

DISCUSSION QUESTIONS

1) What is the theme of "Grin"?
The theme is to not let others see that you are facing adversity, and always grin no matter what you are facing.

2) Reading poetry out loud can often allow us to hear things and see things that we didn't notice while reading in our heads. Reread "Grin" out loud. What differences do you notice about how the poem sounds, how it is structured and what the poet is saying?
Answers will vary.

3) What adversity is the speaker referring to in this poem?
The speaker is referring to the troubles that everyone faces in life.

4) What do you think about the speaker's advice? Do you agree or disagree?
Answers will vary.

FAVORITE LINE

What is your favorite line from "Grin"? Why?
Answers will vary.

ENRICHMENT ACTIVITY

Consider what advice you would give to a friend that is dealing with a difficult situation. What word would you use to represent this advice? Write a poem using this word as your title, and then see how many times you can include the word in your poem.

THE SPELL OF THE YUKON

LESSON 13: THE SHOOTING OF DAN MCGREW

VOCABULARY

Look for these words in your reading:

Dreary – dismal or gloomy
Banished – to drive away
Ghastly – intensely unpleasant
Hooch – a strong alcoholic drink

READING

Read: "The Shooting of Dan McGrew" (Pages 40-43)

DISCUSSION QUESTIONS

1) Who is Dan McGrew? Who is Lou?
Dan McGrew is only described as dangerous. At the beginning of the poem he is sitting in the back of the bar playing solo games as Lou watches. Lou is his girlfriend and she is watching the stranger from the across the room.

2) Who is the third character in the poem? Why does he want to "repay" Dan McGrew?
The third character in the story is described as a stranger. He was a miner who is angry with Dan McGrew for taking Lou from him.

3) What pictures come to mind as you read this poem? Which words or lines inspire these images?
Answers will vary.

4) Do you think that it was necessary for Robert Service to explain what the corpse looked like in such detail? How would the poem be different without this imagery?
Answers will vary. Robert Service was famous for his ability to use imagery in his poetry. Without the description of the corpse, the reader would not visualize the poem in the same way.

FAVORITE LINE

What is your favorite line from "The Shooting of Dan McGrew"? Why?
Answers will vary.

ENRICHMENT ACTIVITY

"The Shooting of Dan McGrew" is one of Robert Service's most well-known poems. It even inspired a movie and a novel. Write a poem that is based on your favorite movie or novel. You can use a single scene or the entire plot as your inspiration. When your poem is finished, read it to a friend or classmate, and see if they can guess which movie or book inspired your poem.

THE SPELL OF THE YUKON

LESSON 14: THE CREMATION OF SAM MCGEE

VOCABULARY

Look for these words in your reading:

Marge – edge
Stern – severity of nature or manner
Loathed – dislike greatly
Derelict – abandoned ship

READING

Read: "The Cremation of Sam McGee" (Pages 44-47)

DISCUSSION QUESTIONS

1) How did Sam McGee die? Who cremated him? Why?
Sam McGee died on the trail, apparently from the cold. He asked the speaker to cremate him, and he kept his promise.

2) How does the speaker describe the Arctic?
It was so cold that your lashes would freeze together if you closed your eyes.

3) What do you think is the theme of this poem?
Answers will vary. Some examples may be: keeping your promise to a friend, death or man's relationship with the wild.

4) What do you think about the ending of the poem? Did you look at the poem differently after reading the ending? Explain your answer.
Answers will vary.

FAVORITE LINE

What is your favorite line from "The Cremation of Sam McGee"? Why?
Answers will vary.

ENRICHMENT ACTIVITY

In "The Cremation of Sam McGee," Robert Service adds humor to the sensitive subject of mortality and death. Write your own funny poem on any topic.

THE SPELL OF THE YUKON

LESSON 15: MY MADONNA

VOCABULARY

Look for these words in your reading:

Haled – compel (someone) to go
Bade – requested to come
Connoisseur – a person qualified to act as a judge in matters of taste and appreciation
Halo – a disk or circle of light shown surrounding or above the head of a saint or holy person to represent their holiness

READING

Read: "My Madonna" (Page 48)

DISCUSSION QUESTIONS

1) Who is the speaker? What does he do?
The speaker is an artist who paints a portrait of a woman on the street.

2) Who is "Madonna" in this poem? Do you think that the connoisseur correctly identified the woman in the painting? Why or why not?
Answers will vary. The connoisseur identified the woman that the speaker painted as the Virgin Mary.

3) What do you notice about the structure of the poem?
This poem is written in alternate rhyme scheme ABAB.

4) How would you describe the mood of this poem?
Answers will vary. Funny or light are two possible examples.

FAVORITE LINE

What is your favorite line from "My Madonna"? Why?

Answers will vary.

ENRICHMENT ACTIVITY

The term "Madonna," when referring to a picture or statue of Mary, dates back to the 17th century, often referencing works from the Italian Renaissance. See if you can find an example of a Madonna painting that fits the description of the poem (halo, babe at her breast, etc.). Search in art books at your local library or online. Write a poem about what you see in that painting.

THE SPELL OF THE YUKON

LESSON 16: UNFORGOTTEN

VOCABULARY

Look for these words in your reading:

Garret – a room or unfinished part of a house just under the roof
Drear – having nothing likely to provide cheer or comfort
Toils – exhausting work
Seer – a person who can supposedly see into the future

READING

Read: "Unforgotten" (Page 49)

DISCUSSION QUESTIONS

1) Describe the woman in the poem.
She lingers in the sunshine, she is more beautiful than lilies and she is a dreamer.

2) Describe the man in the poem.
The man works hard writing in a dreary, dark room, until he gets so tired that he needs to go outside.

3) Why do you think the poem was titled "Unforgotten"?
Answers will vary. One example is that even though the woman and man in the poem are far from each other, they will not forget about each other.

4) "Unforgotten" is written in enclosed rhyme scheme (ABBA). The first and fourth line of each stanza rhyme, and the second and third stanza rhyme. Copy the first stanza below and label the first and fourth line A, and the second and third line B.
I know a garden where the lilies gleam, A
And one who lingers in the sunshine there; B
She is than white-stoled lily far more fair, B
And oh, her eyes are heaven-lit with dream! A

FAVORITE LINE

What is your favorite line from "Unforgotten"? Why?
Answers will vary.

ENRICHMENT ACTIVITY

Could you picture the woman fairer than lilies and the man who toils in a dark garret as you read the poem? If not, read the poem again and try to picture them. Write three stanzas to add to the poem that include a description of the images that you see of the man and woman as you read. Follow the rhyme pattern of this poem (ABBA).

THE SPELL OF THE YUKON

LESSON 17: THE RECKONING

VOCABULARY

Look for these words in your reading:

Reckoning – a settling of accounts
Terrapin – small edible turtle

READING

Read: "The Reckoning" (Pages 50-51)

DISCUSSION QUESTIONS

1) What is the theme of "The Reckoning"?
It is nice to enjoy your life, but be careful how you live because you will face a day of reckoning where you will have to answer for how you spent your life.

2) Did you notice the use of symbolism in this poem? If not, read it again. What does "the bill" symbolize?
The bill symbolizes the consequences of how we spend our life.

3) If you had to give an alternate title to this poem, what would it be?
Answers will vary.

4) How would you describe the tone of this poem (examples: pessimistic, serious, playful)? Explain your answer.
Answers will vary.

FAVORITE LINE

What is your favorite line from "The Reckoning"? Why?

Answers will vary.

ENRICHMENT ACTIVITY

Symbolism in poetry can be expressed in many ways. An object can represent something more significant. For example, a dove can symbolize peace. A word, action or event also can be symbolic. Write a poem that includes some form of symbolism.

THE SPELL OF THE YUKON

LESSON 18: QUATRAINS

VOCABULARY

Look for these words in your reading:

Quatrains – a unit or group of four lines of verse
Marionette – a puppet moved by attached strings or wires
Spheral – perfectly rounded
Astral – related to, or coming from the stars

READING

Read: "Quatrains" (Pages 52-53)

DISCUSSION QUESTIONS

1) Why do you think this poem is titled "Quatrains"?
Each stanza has four lines.

2) What is the difference between the two viewpoints in the poem?
One believes that your life is in your own hands. You have a choice in how your life turns out. The speaker believes we are slaves of circumstance and that we have no choice in how our lives turn out.

3) Which point of view do you most agree with?
Answers will vary.

4) How do you think the woman in the poem might respond to the speaker? Write two or three sentences of prose (not poetry) from her point of view.
Answers will vary.

FAVORITE LINE

What is your favorite line from "Quatrains"? Why?
Answers will vary.

ENRICHMENT ACTIVITY

Write a quatrain poem following an alternate rhyme scheme (ABAB).

Fifth- and seventh-grade students created a puppet show for Chitina school children during the 1930s.

Spell of the Yukon Vocabulary

Crossword Puzzle II

Read the Across and Down clues and fill in the blank boxes that match the number on the clues

ACROSS

1 Compel (someone) to go
4 Exhausting work
5 Close friend or associate
8 A strong alcoholic drink
11 To drive away
13 Requested to come
15 To refuse or check sharply
19 Try to acquire or develop (a quality, sentiment or skill)
21 An authoritative command
22 Perfectly rounded
23 Desolate
24 A person who can supposedly see into the future
25 Abandoned ship
26 A puppet moved by attached strings or wires
27 Dismal or gloomy
28 Intensely unpleasant
29 A settling of accounts

DOWN

1 A disk or circle of light shown surrounding or above the head of a saint or holy person to represent their holiness
2 Dislike greatly
3 Work
4 Small edible turtle
6 To avoid something one ought to do
7 A guard whose job is to stand and keep watch
9 Influence
10 Edge
12 To strike with an open hand
14 A person qualified to act as a judge in matters of taste and appreciation
15 State of repentance (feeling sorry for one's sins)
16 Speak irreverently about God or sacred things
17 Related to, or coming from the stars
18 A unit or group of four lines of verse
20 A room or unfinished part of a house just under the roof
24 Severity of nature or manner

Spell of the Yukon Vocabulary

Crossword Puzzle II Key

Read the Across and Down clues and fill in the blank boxes that match the number on the clues

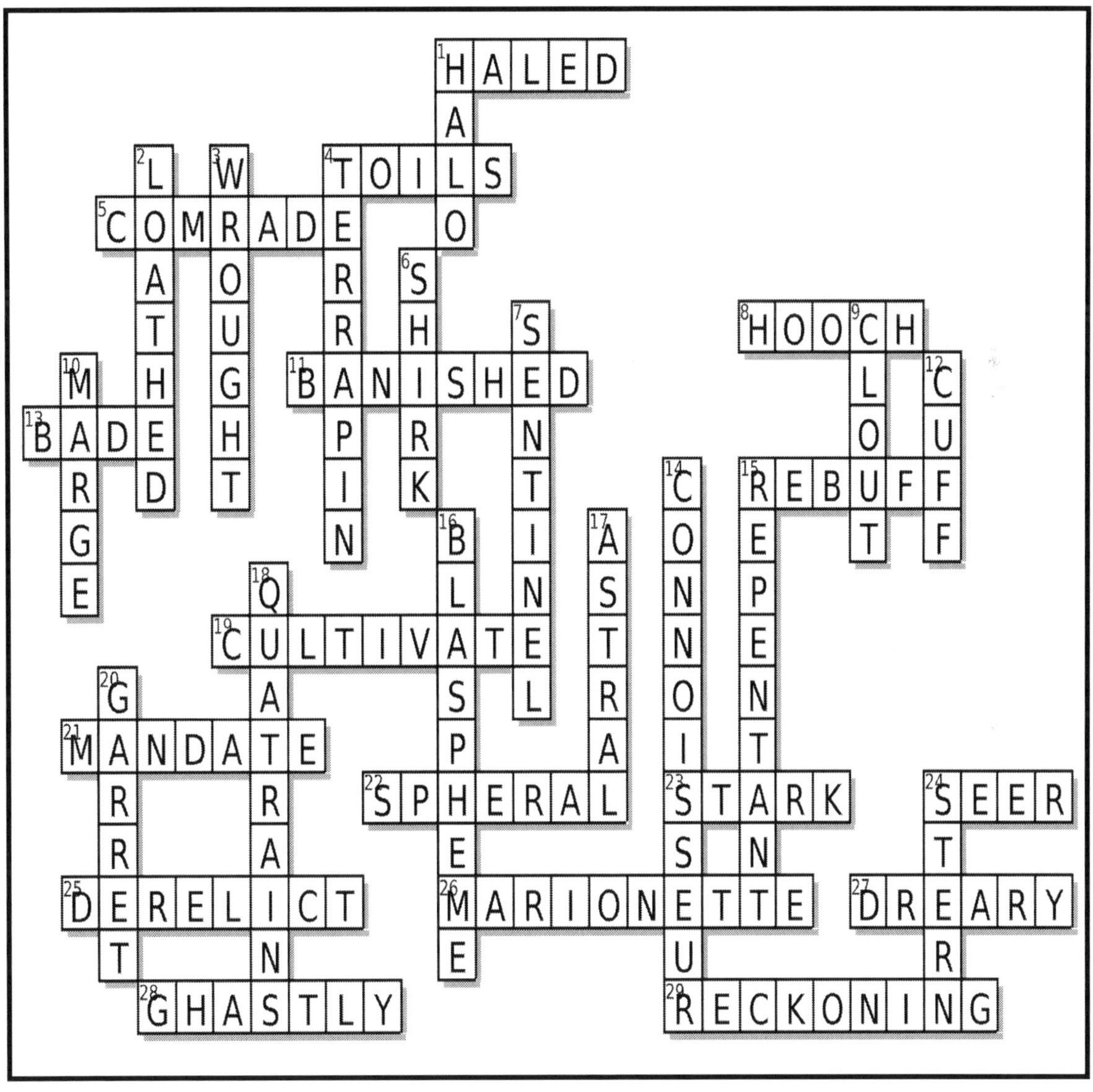

FAVORITE LINE

What is your favorite line from "The Men That Don't Fit In"? Why?
Answers will vary.

ENRICHMENT ACTIVITY

Write a poem from the point of view of a person, animal or object that feels that it doesn't fit in.

THE SPELL OF THE YUKON

LESSON 20: MUSIC IN THE BUSH

VOCABULARY

Look for these words in your reading:

Tremulous – shaking or quivering slightly
Listless – too tired or too little interested to want to do things
Melodious – pleasing to the ear because of melody
Vagrant – a person without a settled home or regular work who wanders from place to place

READING

Read: "Music in the Bush" (Pages 56-57)

DISCUSSION QUESTIONS

1) What are five words to describe the woman in the poem?
Answers will vary. Some examples are: singer, old, sad, prima-donna and lonely.

2) Choose the word that best describes the mood of this poem: romantic, sorrowful or humorous.
Sorrowful

3) How do the words used in this poem affect the mood of the poem?
Words such as sad, mellow, drearily and gloom create a sorrowful mood.

4) What images come to mind as you read this poem?
Answers will vary.

FAVORITE LINE

What is your favorite line from "Music in the Bush"? Why?
Answers will vary.

ENRICHMENT ACTIVITY

Write a poem that expresses one of the following moods: optimistic, sorrowful or humorous.

THE SPELL OF THE YUKON

LESSON 21: RHYME OF THE REMITTANCE MAN

VOCABULARY

Look for these words in your reading:

Remittance – money spent especially in payment
Gilded – covered thinly with gold leaf or gold paint
Vivid – very strong or bright
Rapture – a strong feeling of joy, delight or love

READING

Read: "Rhyme of the Remittance Man" (Pages 58-59)

DISCUSSION QUESTIONS

1) What is the setting of "Rhyme of the Remittance Man"?
A log cabin far away from everything.

2) Who is the speaker?
The speaker is a man who left a life of pursuing business and money in London to live a simple life in a log cabin.

3) Explain what the following line means: "He is one of us no longer — let him be."
The speaker is telling the audience that he would rather live a simple life in nature than to be considered a success by the standards of those he left behind in the busy city.

4) What do you think about this poem? Did you enjoy it? Why or why not?
Answers will vary.

FAVORITE LINE

What is your favorite line from "Rhyme of the Remittance Man"? Why?
Answers will vary.

ENRICHMENT ACTIVITY

Paraphrase "Rhyme of the Remittance Man" in one or two paragraphs for someone who has not read the poem. Include all of the important details in your own words.

THE SPELL OF THE YUKON

LESSON 22: THE LOW-DOWN WHITE

VOCABULARY

Look for these words in your reading:

Haggard – very thin especially from great hunger, worry or pain
Squalid – extremely dirty and unpleasant
Rogue – a mischievous individual
Bleak – dreary

READING

Read: "The Low-Down White" (Pages 60-61)

DISCUSSION QUESTIONS

1) Do you think that the speaker in this poem is happy with his life? Why or why not?
The speaker is not happy with his life. He wants to forget who he is and the man that he used to be.

2) How would you describe the tone of "The Low-Down White"?
Answers will vary. The tone is somber.

3) What rhyme scheme is used in this poem?
Alternate rhyme scheme.

4) What did you think about this poem? Did you enjoy it? Why or why not?
Answers will vary.

FAVORITE LINE

What is your favorite line from "The Low-Down White"? Why?
Answers will vary.

ENRICHMENT ACTIVITY

What are your three favorite poems (either from this class or elsewhere)? What elements do your favorite poems have in common? Do you relate to the subject matter in some way? Are there similarities in the structure, pattern or tone of the poems? Write your answers below.

THE SPELL OF THE YUKON

LESSON 23: THE LITTLE OLD LOG CABIN

VOCABULARY

Look for these words in your reading:

Gouges – to cut holes or grooves in with or as if with a gouge
Solemn – being serious and dignified in appearance or behavior

READING

Read: "The Little Old Log Cabin" (Pages 62-63)

DISCUSSION QUESTIONS

1) Did you have any difficulty understanding "The Little Old Log Cabin"? What are some things that you can do to make a poem easier to understand?
Read the poem out loud. When dialect is difficult to understand, you can rewrite the poem without the dialect.

2) How does the dialect affect the meaning and tone of the poem?
The dialect adds authenticity to the poem and gives the impression that the speaker is a native of the Northland.

3) What does the little old log cabin represent to the speaker?
The log cabin represents a place of safety, quiet and refuge.

4) In what ways can you relate to this poem?
Answers will vary.

THE SPELL OF THE YUKON

LESSON 24: THE YOUNGER SON

VOCABULARY

Look for these words in your reading:

Stalwart – marked by outstanding strength and vigor of mind, body or spirit
Sombre – dismal, gloomy, sad
Argent – resembling silver
In the lurch – leave in a vulnerable and unsupported position

READING

Read: "The Younger Son" (Pages 65-67)

DISCUSSION QUESTIONS

1) In what continent does "The Younger Son" take place? Hint: Look for clues in the first stanza on Page 66.
Australia. There also is mention of New Zealand and Vancouver.

2) Describe the younger son.
The younger son is "bronzed and stalwart." "A child of nature, fearless, frank, and free." He is welcoming, warm and kind-hearted. He is enjoying his life in other countries.

3) How does the speaker feel about the younger son?
Answers will vary. The speaker thinks very highly of the younger son. He is proud of him.

4) Which image in the poem stands out to you the most? Why?
Answers will vary.

FAVORITE LINE

What is your favorite line from "The Younger Son"? Why?
Answers will vary.

ENRICHMENT ACTIVITY

Write a poem from the point of view of the younger son. Consider how he might feel about his life. Consider what he might say to his family in England.

THE SPELL OF THE YUKON

LESSON 25: THE MARCH OF THE DEAD

VOCABULARY

Look for these words in your reading:

Triumph – a military victory or conquest
Bunting – a thin cloth used chiefly for making flags and patriotic decorations
Gaunt – lean and haggard, especially because of suffering, hunger, or age
Writhing – to twist and turn this way and that

READING

Read: "The March of the Dead" (Pages 68-70)

DISCUSSION QUESTIONS

1) What is the theme of "The March of the Dead."
The theme is to remember those that died during war.

2) How would you describe this poem to someone that hasn't read it?
"The March of the Dead" is about a man watching soldiers return home from battle. He and the crowd are cheering in triumph until the army of the dead come to remind everyone that they paid with their lives to win the war. The speaker realizes that he was daydreaming and will never forget those that died in battle.

3) How does the use of imagery affect the meaning and tone of this poem?
Answers will vary. Robert Service uses vivid pictures to describe the army of the dead. The descriptions changed the tone of the poem from cheerful to gloomy.

4) How did you feel after reading this poem? What words describe your emotions?
Answers will vary.

FAVORITE LINE

What is your favorite line from "The March of the Dead"? Why?
Answers will vary.

ENRICHMENT ACTIVITY

Write a poem that changes tone. For example, your poem can begin with a humorous tone and shift to a serious tone. Focus on using imagery to create your intended tones.

THE SPELL OF THE YUKON

LESSON 26: 'FIGHTING MAC' A LIFE TRAGEDY

VOCABULARY

Look for these words in your reading:

Spectre – something that bothers the mind
Pibroch – a set of variations for the Scottish bagpipe
Flouts – ignore or disregard
Rapine – the violent seizure of someone's property

READING

Read: "'Fighting Mac' A Life Tragedy" (Pages 71-73)

DISCUSSION QUESTIONS

1) Why do you think that Robert Service titled the poem "A Life Tragedy"?
This poem is about a war hero who committed suicide.

2) What do you notice about the rhyme scheme of this poem?
In most stanzas, the poet uses alternate rhyme scheme and the last two lines rhyme.

3) Alliteration is a literary device in which a number of words begin with the same consonant sound close together. It adds musical effect to the work that makes it more pleasurable to read. Here's one example from William Shakespeare's Romeo and Juliet: "From forth the fatal loins of these two foes; a pair of star-cross'd lovers take their life." Shakespeare's repeated use of fs and ls in these lines is an example of alliteration.

What are two examples of alliteration in "'Fighting Mac' A Life Tragedy"?
"A last defiance to dark Death is hurled," "Alone he falls, with wide, wan, woeful eyes," "The burn brawls darkly down the shaggy glen," "He sees himself a barefoot boy again, Bending o'er page of legendary lore." "He sees the ravaged ranks"

4) In what ways can you relate to this poem?
Answers will vary.

FAVORITE LINE

What is your favorite line from "'Fighting Mac' A Life Tragedy"? Why?
Answers will vary.

ENRICHMENT ACTIVITY

Understanding the historical places, events and people referenced in a poem can help you understand the meaning of the poem. Take some time to research the following list of people and events and write your notes below.

1) Fighting Mac 2) Rob Roy 3) Roderick Dhu 4) Boer War 5) Battle of Magersfontein

After your research, reread the poem. Did you gain greater insight into the meaning of the poem?

THE SPELL OF THE YUKON

LESSON 27: THE WOMAN AND THE ANGEL

VOCABULARY

Look for these words in your reading:

Doffed – to remove or take off
Celestial – of relating to, or suggesting heaven
Scruples – a moral consideration or rule of conduct that makes one uneasy or makes action difficult
Beguiled – deceived by cunning means

READING

Read: "The Woman and the Angel" (Pages 74-75)

DISCUSSION QUESTIONS

1) What did you think that poem was about after you read the title? How did this compare to what the poem really was about?
Answers will vary.

2) Summarize "The Woman and the Angel" in one sentence.
Answers will vary. "The Woman and the Angel" is about an angel who leaves heaven because he is bored, only find that those on earth have lost their morality.

3) What do you notice about the rhyme scheme of this poem?
The first two lines of each stanza rhyme and the last two lines of each stanza rhyme. This is called the couplet rhyme scheme (AABB).

4) Can you draw any conclusions about the poet's feelings about human morality from this poem?
Answers will vary. From this poem, we can infer that he believes that many are following a sinful path, rather than a moral path.

FAVORITE LINE

What is your favorite line from "The Woman and the Angel"? Why?
Answers will vary.

ENRICHMENT ACTIVITY

"The Woman and the Angel" is an example of a couplet (AABB) rhyme scheme. Write your own poem that follows this rhyme scheme.

THE SPELL OF THE YUKON

LESSON 28: THE RHYME OF THE RESTLESS ONES

VOCABULARY

Look for these words in your reading:

Stagnation – to become motionless
Roam – to go from place to place without purpose or direction
Serf – a slave bound to a certain piece of land
Blot out – to make obscure, insignificant or inconsequential

READING

Read: "The Rhyme of the Restless Ones" (Pages 76-77)

DISCUSSION QUESTIONS

1) Describe the "restless ones" in your own words.
Answers will vary.

2) Which Robert Service poem has a similar theme to "The Rhyme of the Restless Ones"?
The Men Who Don't Fit In.

3) Explain the following stanza in your own words:

> No, there's that in us that time can never tame;
> And life will always seem a careless game;
> And they'd better far forget —
> Those who say they love us yet —
> Forget, blot out with bitterness our name.

Answers will vary. The restless ones live a life of adventure without a plan or goal. They live to enjoy life and don't like to stay in one place. It is better for those that love them to forget about them.

4) In what ways do you relate to this poem?
Answers will vary.

FAVORITE LINE

What is your favorite line from "The Rhyme of the Restless Ones"? Why?
Answers will vary.

ENRICHMENT ACTIVITY

"The Rhyme of the Restless Ones" is an example of a couplet (AABB) rhyme scheme. Write a poem about a time that you felt restless. Incorporate at least two of the vocabulary words from this lesson into your poem.

THE SPELL OF THE YUKON

LESSON 29: NEW YEAR'S EVE

VOCABULARY

Look for these words in your reading:

Weltering – moving in a turbulent fashion
Ghastly – horrible or shocking
Sodden – dull or lacking in expression
Rouse – to bring out of a state of sleep, unconsciousness, inactivity

READING

Read: "New Year's Eve" (Pages 78-81)

DISCUSSION QUESTIONS

1) Read the poem out loud again. Did you notice anything new that you didn't notice the first time that you read it? If so, what?
Answers will vary.

2) Are there any instances of anaphora in this poem? If so, which words were repeated?
They'll, And, Don't you remember.

3) What word best describes the tone of this poem: humorous, serious or gloomy? What are some phrases that support your answer?
The tone can be described as serious or gloomy. "dark and drear," "Shuffling along in the icy wind, ghastly and gaunt and slow," "'Twere better to die a thousand deaths than live each day as I live!"

4) How did this poem make you feel?
Answers will vary.

FAVORITE LINE

What is your favorite line from "New Year's Eve"? Why?
Answers will vary.

ENRICHMENT ACTIVITY

New Year's Eve is typically a time of reflection and making resolutions for the future. Write your own New Year's Eve poem that either reflects on your past or expresses your hopes for the future.

THE SPELL OF THE YUKON

LESSON 30: COMFORT

VOCABULARY

Look for these words in your reading:

Bereft – not having something needed, wanted or expected
Dazzles – blind temporarily
Mope – be dejected and apathetic
Tatters – irregularly torn pieces of cloth

READING

Read: "Comfort" (Pages 82)

DISCUSSION QUESTIONS

1) What is the theme of "Comfort"?
The theme of "Comfort" is that no matter how difficult things in your life may be, you still have the beauty of nature, God and love, so you will be okay.

2) Who is the audience of this poem?
The audience is those who think that life is against them.

3) Do you agree with the speaker's advice? Why or why not?
Answers will vary.

4) What words or phrases stand out to you the most? Why?
Answers will vary.

FAVORITE LINE

What is your favorite line from "Comfort"? Why?
Answers will vary.

ENRICHMENT ACTIVITY

Poetry can be used to uplift and encourage your readers. Think of a time that a friend or family member was going through a difficult time. Write a poem to encourage that person.

THE SPELL OF THE YUKON

LESSON 31: THE HARPY

VOCABULARY

Look for these words in your reading:

Harpy – slang term for a lady of the night
Iniquity – something that is unjust or wicked; sin
Sate – satisfy (a desire or an appetite) to the fullest
Attainted – affect or infect with disease or corruption

READING

Read: "The Harpy" (Pages 83-85)

DISCUSSION QUESTIONS

1) Why do you think that Robert Service titled this poem "The Harpy"?
This poem is about a woman who is a lady of the night.

2) Summarize the poem in one sentence.
Answers will vary. "The Harpy" is about a woman who is a prostitute, and she believes that she was destined to live a life of sin.

3) How does the rhyme scheme affect the tone and meaning of this poem?
This poem contains short stanzas of three lines that all rhyme (AAA BBB). This is called triplet rhyme scheme.

4) Do you think the woman described in this poem is happy? Explain your answer.
Answers will vary.

FAVORITE LINE

What is your favorite line from "The Harpy"? Why?
Answers will vary.

ENRICHMENT ACTIVITY

"The Harpy" has a triplet rhyme scheme where every stanza contains three lines that rhyme (AAA). Write a poem that contains at least one stanza of three lines that rhyme.

THE SPELL OF THE YUKON

LESSON 32: PREMONITION

VOCABULARY

Look for these words in your reading:

Premonition – a forewarning
Gibbous – more than half but less than fully illuminated

READING

Read: "Premonition" (Page 86)

DISCUSSION QUESTIONS

1) What is the theme of "Premonition"?
The theme of "Premonition" is death.

2) Who had a premonition? Who was the premonition about?
The speaker had a premonition about the woman he loved dying a year before she died.

3) What line in this poem contains a metaphor (a figure of speech that compares two things that are unrelated but share common characteristics).
Line 4: And the voice of my sweet was a silver bell.

4) Have you ever had a premonition? If so, explain.
Answers will vary.

FAVORITE LINE

What is your favorite line from "Premonition"? Why?
Answers will vary.

ENRICHMENT ACTIVITY

Metaphors and similes are two literary devices that are often confused:

Metaphor: a figure of speech that compares two things that are unrelated but share common characteristics without the use of "like" or "as"

Simile: a figure of speech which explicitly compares two things that are unrelated using the words "like" or "as"

Write two examples of a metaphor and two examples of a simile from any kind of literature. Then write your own example of a metaphor and a simile.

THE SPELL OF THE YUKON

LESSON 33: THE TRAMPS

VOCABULARY

Look for these words in your reading:

Comrade – an intimate friend or associate
Vassal – someone/something that is subordinate
Jest – a comic act or remark
Exultantly – full of or expressing joy or triumph

READING

Read: "The Tramps" (Page 87)

DISCUSSION QUESTIONS

1) What is the theme of "The Tramps"?
Answers will vary. The theme of "The Tramps" is adventure.

2) Who is the speaker of this poem? Who is the audience?
The speaker is an adventurer who left his home to travel to start a new life in a new land many years ago. The audience is those who did the same.

3) Where do you think the "road to Anywhere" leads?
Answers will vary. The road to Anywhere could lead to gold rush lands.

4) In what ways can you relate to this poem? Explain why.
Answers will vary.

FAVORITE LINE

What is your favorite line from "The Tramps"? Why?
Answers will vary.

ENRICHMENT ACTIVITY

Write a poem with the theme of adventure. Include at least two of the vocabulary words from this lesson.

THE SPELL OF THE YUKON

LESSON 34: L'ENVOI

VOCABULARY

Look for these words in your reading:

L'envoi – one or more detached verses at the end of a literary composition, serving to convey the moral, or to address the poem to a particular person
Assail – to attack violently with words or blows
Argonauts – a group of heroes who accompanied Jason on board the ship *Argo* in the quest for the Golden Fleece
Vanquishing – to defeat and gain control of completely

READING

Read: "L'envoi" (Pages 88-89)

DISCUSSION QUESTIONS

1) What is the purpose of this poem?
The purpose of this poem is to let the audience know who his songs are for – adventurers on the trail.

2) What rhyme scheme does Robert Service use in the poem?
Alternate rhyme scheme (ABAB).

3) What literary devices do you notice in the first stanza of this poem?
Anaphora is used in lines 1-4. The poet repeats the words "you are" at the beginning of each line. Lines 7 and 8 contain similes.

4) What images came to mind as you read this poem? What words or phrases inspired these images?
Answers will vary.

FAVORITE LINE

What is your favorite line from "L'envoi"? Why?
Answers will vary.

ENRICHMENT ACTIVITY

You have now read and analyzed 34 poems by Robert Service. Which one was your favorite? Why? Look over the poems that you wrote for enrichment activities. Which one is your favorite? Why? Write your answers below.

Courtesy Wikipedia

Robert Service

Spell of the Yukon Vocabulary

Crossword Puzzle III

Read the Across and Down clues and fill in the blank boxes that match the number on the clues

ACROSS

2 Very strong or bright
4 Ignore or disregard
7 Someone/something that is subordinate
9 Not having something needed, wanted or expected
12 An intimate friend or associate
15 Be dejected and apathetic
17 A strong feeling of joy, delight or love
18 A slave bound to a certain piece of land
20 Very thin, especially from great hunger, worry or pain
21 Horrible or shocking
25 Marked by outstanding strength and vigor of mind, body or spirit
26 Dull or lacking in expression
28 Too tired or too little interested to want to do things
30 Covered thinly with gold leaf or gold paint
35 To bring out of a state of sleep, unconsciousness, inactivity
36 Affect or infect with disease or corruption
38 The most active, thriving or satisfying stage or period
40 Resembling silver
41 Shaking or quivering slightly
42 Leave in a vulnerable and unsupported position
44 To become motionless
46 Dreary
47 More than half but less than fully illuminated
48 Familiar friends, neighbors or relatives
49 A mischievous individual
50 Of relating to, or suggesting heaven
51 A military victory or conquest
52 A set of variations for the Scottish bagpipe
53 Slang term for a lady of the night
54 Something that bothers the mind
55 To defeat and gain control of completely

DOWN

1 The violent seizure of someone's property
3 To remove or take off
5 Irregularly torn pieces of cloth
6 To go from place to place without purpose or direction
8 Being serious and dignified in appearance or behavior
10 A moral consideration or rule of conduct that makes one uneasy or makes action difficult
11 Blind temporarily
13 A person without a settled home or regular work who wanders from place to place
14 Deceived by cunning means
16 To attack violently with words or blows
19 Extremely dirty and unpleasant
22 A group of heroes who accompanied Jason on board the ship Argo in the quest for the Golden Fleece
23 Pleasing to the ear because of melody
24 One or more detached verses at the end of a literary composition, serving to convey the moral, or to address the poem to a particular person
27 Moving in a turbulent fashion
29 Dismal, gloomy, sad
30 To cut holes or grooves in with or as if with a gouge
31 Something that is unjust or wicked; sin
32 To twist and turn this way and that
33 Lean and haggard, especially because of suffering, hunger, or age
34 A comic act or remark
37 Full of or expressing joy or triumph

Spell of the Yukon Vocabulary

Crossword Puzzle III Key

Read the Across and Down clues and fill in the blank boxes that match the number on the clues

DOWN - Continued

38 A forewarning
39 Money spent especially in payment
43 Satisfy (a desire or an appetite) to the fullest
45 A thin cloth used chiefly for making flags and patriotic decorations
46 To make obscure, insignificant or inconsequential

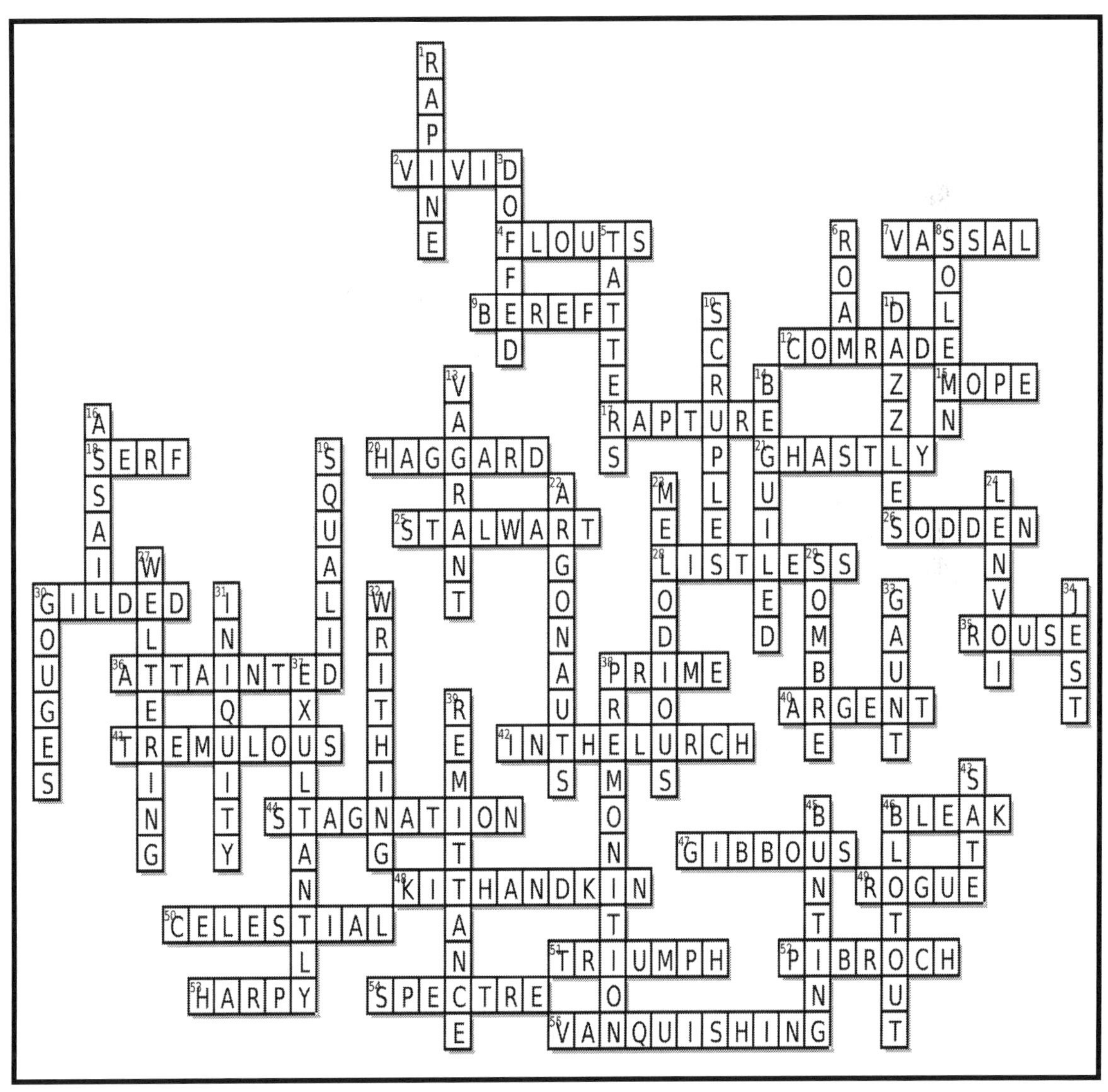

THE SPELL OF THE YUKON

LESSON 35: BARD OF THE YUKON/AFTER THE YUKON

READING

"Bard of the Yukon" (Pages 90-103)
"Life After the Yukon" (Pages 104-114)

ESSAY QUESTIONS

Answer the following questions in paragraph form:

1) What were Robert Service's early years like? How did those expeiences influence his writing?
Answers will vary.

2) How and why did Robert Service end up in Alaska? How did his time in the Yukon become a turning point in his life? In what ways did it inspire his writing?
Answers will vary.

3) After reading about the life of Robert Service, what new insights did you gain into his poetry?

Answers will vary.

How to grade the assignments

Our rubric grids are designed to make it easy for you to grade your students' poems and essays. Encourage your students to look at the grid before completing an assignment as a reminder of what an exemplary poem should include.

You can mark grades for discussion questions, favorite line questions, and enrichment assignments on the last page of each lesson in the student workbook. Use these pages as a tool to help your students track their progress and improve their assignment grades.

Discussion Questions

Discussion questions test the students' ability to explain and discuss important themes in the assigned reading. Students are given 10 points for every correct answer. You can give 5 points for partial credit. Mark these points on the last page of each lesson in the student workbook.

Enrichment Activities (Poetry)

The majority of the enrichment activities will instruct students to write an original poem based on the assigned reading.

Students are graded for each poetry enrichment assignment on a scale of 2-10 in five categories:

1) Originality and creativity
2) Following directions
3) Language and style
4) Neatness
5) Grammar and spelling

Use the rubric grid as a guide to give up to 10 points in each category.

Enrichment Activities (Not Poetry)

For enrichment assignments that do not require the student to write an original poem, (Lessons 11, 21, 22, 26, and 32) you can grade the assignment as follows:

50 points = An excellent answer that follows directions completely
40 points = A good answer
30 points = Needs work

Mark these points for each enrichment assignment on the last page of each unit in the student workbook.

LESSON 1: THE LAND GOD FORGOT

Discussion Questions ______ (10 pts. per question – possible 40 pts.)
Favorite Quote ______ (possible 10 pts.)

Enrichment Activity

Originality and Creativity	______	(possible 10 pts.)
Follows Directions	______	(possible 10 pts.)
Language and Style	______	(possible 10 pts.)
Composition is Neat	______	(possible 10 pts.)
Grammar and Spelling	______	(possible 10 pts.)

Total Points ________

LESSON 2: THE SPELL OF THE YUKON

Discussion Questions ______ (10 pts. per question – possible 50 pts.)
Favorite Quote (No points for this lesson)

Enrichment Activity

Originality and Creativity	______	(possible 10 pts.)
Follows Directions	______	(possible 10 pts.)
Language and Style	______	(possible 10 pts.)
Composition is Neat	______	(possible 10 pts.)
Grammar and Spelling	______	(possible 10 pts.)

Total Points ________

LESSON 3: THE HEART OF THE SOURDOUGH

Discussion Questions ______ (10 pts. per question – possible 40 pts.)
Favorite Quote ______ (possible 10 pts.)

Enrichment Activity

Originality and Creativity	______	(possible 10 pts.)
Follows Directions	______	(possible 10 pts.)
Language and Style	______	(possible 10 pts.)
Composition is Neat	______	(possible 10 pts.)
Grammar and Spelling	______	(possible 10 pts.)

Total Points ________

LESSON 4: THE THREE VOICES

Discussion Questions ______ (10 pts. per question – possible 40 pts.)
Favorite Quote ______ (possible 10 pts.)

Enrichment Activity

Originality and Creativity	______ (possible 10 pts.)
Follows Directions	______ (possible 10 pts.)
Language and Style	______ (possible 10 pts.)
Composition is Neat	______ (possible 10 pts.)
Grammar and Spelling	______ (possible 10 pts.)

Total Points ________

LESSON 5: THE LAW OF THE YUKON

Discussion Questions ______ (10 pts. per question – possible 40 pts.)
Favorite Quote ______ (possible 10 pts.)

Enrichment Activity

Originality and Creativity	______ (possible 10 pts.)
Follows Directions	______ (possible 10 pts.)
Language and Style	______ (possible 10 pts.)
Composition is Neat	______ (possible 10 pts.)
Grammar and Spelling	______ (possible 10 pts.)

Total Points ________

LESSON 6: THE PARSON'S LAW

Discussion Questions ______ (10 pts. per question – possible 40 pts.)
Favorite Quote ______ (possible 10 pts.)

Enrichment Activity

Originality and Creativity	______ (possible 10 pts.)
Follows Directions	______ (possible 10 pts.)
Language and Style	______ (possible 10 pts.)
Composition is Neat	______ (possible 10 pts.)
Grammar and Spelling	______ (possible 10 pts.)

Total Points ________

LESSON 7: THE CALL OF THE WILD

Discussion Questions ______ (10 pts. per question – possible 40 pts.)
Favorite Quote ______ (possible 10 pts.)

Enrichment Activity

Originality and Creativity	______	(possible 10 pts.)
Follows Directions	______	(possible 10 pts.)
Language and Style	______	(possible 10 pts.)
Composition is Neat	______	(possible 10 pts.)
Grammar and Spelling	______	(possible 10 pts.)

Total Points ________

LESSON 8: THE LONE TRAIL

Discussion Questions ______ (10 pts. per question – possible 40 pts.)
Favorite Quote ______ (possible 10 pts.)

Enrichment Activity

Originality and Creativity	______	(possible 10 pts.)
Follows Directions	______	(possible 10 pts.)
Language and Style	______	(possible 10 pts.)
Composition is Neat	______	(possible 10 pts.)
Grammar and Spelling	______	(possible 10 pts.)

Total Points ________

LESSON 9: THE PINES

Discussion Questions ______ (10 pts. per question – possible 40 pts.)
Favorite Quote ______ (possible 10 pts.)

Enrichment Activity

Originality and Creativity	______	(possible 10 pts.)
Follows Directions	______	(possible 10 pts.)
Language and Style	______	(possible 10 pts.)
Composition is Neat	______	(possible 10 pts.)
Grammar and Spelling	______	(possible 10 pts.)

Total Points ________

LESSON 10: THE LURE OF LITTLE VOICES

Discussion Questions ______ (10 pts. per question – possible 40 pts.)
Favorite Quote ______ (possible 10 pts.)

Enrichment Activity

Originality and Creativity	______	(possible 10 pts.)
Follows Directions	______	(possible 10 pts.)
Language and Style	______	(possible 10 pts.)
Composition is Neat	______	(possible 10 pts.)
Grammar and Spelling	______	(possible 10 pts.)

Total Points ________

LESSON 11: THE SONG OF THE WAGE-SLAVE

Discussion Questions ______ (10 pts. per question – possible 40 pts.)
Favorite Quote ______ (possible 10 pts.)

Enrichment Activity _____ (possible 50 pts.)

Total Points ________

LESSON 12: GRIN

Discussion Questions ______ (10 pts. per question – possible 40 pts.)
Favorite Quote ______ (possible 10 pts.)

Enrichment Activity

Originality and Creativity	______	(possible 10 pts.)
Follows Directions	______	(possible 10 pts.)
Language and Style	______	(possible 10 pts.)
Composition is Neat	______	(possible 10 pts.)
Grammar and Spelling	______	(possible 10 pts.)

Total Points ________

LESSON 19: THE MEN THAT DON'T FIT IN

Discussion Questions ______ (10 pts. per question – possible 40 pts.)
Favorite Quote ______ (possible 10 pts.)

Enrichment Activity

Originality and Creativity	______	(possible 10 pts.)
Follows Directions	______	(possible 10 pts.)
Language and Style	______	(possible 10 pts.)
Composition is Neat	______	(possible 10 pts.)
Grammar and Spelling	______	(possible 10 pts.)

Total Points ________

LESSON 20: MUSIC IN THE BUSH

Discussion Questions ______ (10 pts. per question – possible 40 pts.)
Favorite Quote ______ (possible 10 pts.)

Enrichment Activity

Originality and Creativity	______	(possible 10 pts.)
Follows Directions	______	(possible 10 pts.)
Language and Style	______	(possible 10 pts.)
Composition is Neat	______	(possible 10 pts.)
Grammar and Spelling	______	(possible 10 pts.)

Total Points ________

LESSON 21: RHYME OF THE REMITTANCE MAN

Discussion Questions ______ (10 pts. per question – possible 40 pts.)
Favorite Quote ______ (possible 10 pts.)
Enrichment Activity (possible 50 pts.)

Total Points ________

LESSON 22: THE LOW-DOWN WHITE

Discussion Questions ______ (10 pts. per question – possible 40 pts.)
Favorite Quote ______ (possible 10 pts.)
Enrichment Activity _____ (possible 50 pts.)

Total Points ________

LESSON 23: THE LITTLE OLD LOG CABIN

Discussion Questions ______ (10 pts. per question – possible 40 pts.)
Favorite Quote ______ (possible 10 pts.)

Enrichment Activity

Originality and Creativity	______ (possible 10 pts.)
Follows Directions	______ (possible 10 pts.)
Language and Style	______ (possible 10 pts.)
Composition is Neat	______ (possible 10 pts.)
Grammar and Spelling	______ (possible 10 pts.)

Total Points ________

LESSON 24: THE YOUNGER SON

Discussion Questions ______ (10 pts. per question – possible 40 pts.)
Favorite Quote ______ (possible 10 pts.)

Enrichment Activity

Originality and Creativity	______ (possible 10 pts.)
Follows Directions	______ (possible 10 pts.)
Language and Style	______ (possible 10 pts.)
Composition is Neat	______ (possible 10 pts.)
Grammar and Spelling	______ (possible 10 pts.)

Total Points ________

LESSON 25: THE MARCH OF THE DEAD

Discussion Questions ______ (10 pts. per question – possible 40 pts.)
Favorite Quote ______ (possible 10 pts.)

Enrichment Activity

Originality and Creativity	______	(possible 10 pts.)
Follows Directions	______	(possible 10 pts.)
Language and Style	______	(possible 10 pts.)
Composition is Neat	______	(possible 10 pts.)
Grammar and Spelling	______	(possible 10 pts.)

Total Points ________

LESSON 26: 'FIGHTING MAC' A LIFE TRAGEDY

Discussion Questions ______ (10 pts. per question – possible 40 pts.)
Favorite Quote ______ (possible 10 pts.)
Enrichment Activity ______ (possible 50 pts.)

Total Points ________

LESSON 27: THE WOMAN AND THE ANGEL

Discussion Questions ______ (10 pts. per question – possible 40 pts.)
Favorite Quote ______ (possible 10 pts.)

Enrichment Activity

Originality and Creativity	______	(possible 10 pts.)
Follows Directions	______	(possible 10 pts.)
Language and Style	______	(possible 10 pts.)
Composition is Neat	______	(possible 10 pts.)
Grammar and Spelling	______	(possible 10 pts.)

Total Points ________

LESSON 28: THE RHYME OF THE RESTLESS ONES

Discussion Questions ______ (10 pts. per question – possible 40 pts.)
Favorite Quote ______ (possible 10 pts.)

Enrichment Activity

Originality and Creativity	______	(possible 10 pts.)
Follows Directions	______	(possible 10 pts.)
Language and Style	______	(possible 10 pts.)
Composition is Neat	______	(possible 10 pts.)
Grammar and Spelling	______	(possible 10 pts.)

Total Points ________

LESSON 29: NEW YEAR'S EVE

Discussion Questions ______ (10 pts. per question – possible 40 pts.)
Favorite Quote ______ (possible 10 pts.)

Enrichment Activity

Originality and Creativity	______	(possible 10 pts.)
Follows Directions	______	(possible 10 pts.)
Language and Style	______	(possible 10 pts.)
Composition is Neat	______	(possible 10 pts.)
Grammar and Spelling	______	(possible 10 pts.)

Total Points ________

LESSON 30: COMFORT

Discussion Questions ______ (10 pts. per question – possible 40 pts.)
Favorite Quote ______ (possible 10 pts.)

Enrichment Activity

Originality and Creativity	______	(possible 10 pts.)
Follows Directions	______	(possible 10 pts.)
Language and Style	______	(possible 10 pts.)
Composition is Neat	______	(possible 10 pts.)
Grammar and Spelling	______	(possible 10 pts.)

Total Points ________

LESSON 31: THE HARPY

Discussion Questions ______ (10 pts. per question – possible 40 pts.)
Favorite Quote ______ (possible 10 pts.)

Enrichment Activity

Originality and Creativity	______	(possible 10 pts.)
Follows Directions	______	(possible 10 pts.)
Language and Style	______	(possible 10 pts.)
Composition is Neat	______	(possible 10 pts.)
Grammar and Spelling	______	(possible 10 pts.)

Total Points ________

LESSON 32: PREMONITION

Discussion Questions ______ (10 pts. per question – possible 40 pts.)
Favorite Quote ______ (possible 10 pts.)
Enrichment Activity _____ (possible 50 pts.)

Total Points ________

LESSON 33: THE TRAMPS

Discussion Questions ______ (10 pts. per question – possible 40 pts.)
Favorite Quote ______ (possible 10 pts.)

Enrichment Activity

Originality and Creativity	______	(possible 10 pts.)
Follows Directions	______	(possible 10 pts.)
Language and Style	______	(possible 10 pts.)
Composition is Neat	______	(possible 10 pts.)
Grammar and Spelling	______	(possible 10 pts.)

Total Points ________

LESSON 34: L'ENVOI

Discussion Questions ______ (10 pts. per question – possible 40 pts.)
Favorite Quote ______ (possible 10 pts.)
Enrichment Activity _____ (possible 50 pts.)

Total Points ________

LESSON 35: THE BARD OF THE YUKON/AFTER THE YUKON

Lesson 35 contains three essay questions to test your students' knowledge of the assigned reading. You can give a student up to 20 points for each essay. Students are graded on a scale of 1-5 in four categories:

1) Understanding the topic
2) Answering all questions completely and accurately
3) Neatness and organization
4) Grammar, spelling and punctuation

Use the essay rubric grid as a guide to give up to 5 points in each category for every essay. Mark these points for each essay on the last page of each unit in the student workbook.

Essay 1

Demonstrates understanding of the topic ______ (possible 5 pts.)
Answered the questions completely and accurately ______ (possible 5 pts.)
Composition is neat ______ (possible 5 pts.)
Grammar and Spelling ______ (possible 5 pts.)

Essay 2

Demonstrates understanding of the topic ______ (possible 5 pts.)
Answered the questions completely and accurately ______ (possible 5 pts.)
Composition is neat ______ (possible 5 pts.)
Grammar and Spelling ______ (possible 5 pts.)

Essay 3

Demonstrates understanding of the topic ______ (possible 5 pts.)
Answered the questions completely and accurately ______ (possible 5 pts.)
Composition is neat ______ (possible 5 pts.)
Grammar and Spelling ______ (possible 5 pts.)

Made in the USA
Columbia, SC
10 February 2023

11593697R00076